WISE QUOTES: MARCUS AURELIUS

(459 MARCUS AURELIUS QUOTES)

Rowan Stevens

'A fool cannot be convinced or even compelled to renounce his folly.' God save me from fools with a little philosophy – no one is more difficult to reach.

'But I get to wear a crown of gold.' If you have your heart set on wearing crowns, why not make one out of roses – you will look even more elegant in that.

'I will throw you into prison.' Correction – it is my body you will throw there.

'My brother is unfair to me.' Well then, keep up your side of the relationship; don't concern yourself with his behaviour, only with what you must do to keep your will in tune with nature.

*'Well, what will my profession in the community be?'
Whatever position you are equipped to fill, so long as
you preserve the man of trust and integrity.*

*"A cucumber is bitter." Throw it away. "There are briars
in the road." Turn aside from them. This is enough. Do
not add, "And why were such things made in the world?"*

*"I am unhappy, because this has happened to me." Not
so: say, "I am happy, though this has happened to me,
because I continue free from pain, neither crushed by
the present nor fearing the future."*

*"It's unfortunate that this has happened". No. It's
fortunate that this has happened and I've remained
unharmed by it — not shattered by the present or
frightened of the future. It could have happened to
anyone. But not everyone could have remained
unharmed by it.*

There is no man so fortunate that there shall not be by him when he is dying some who are pleased with what is going to happen.

A boxer derives the greatest advantage from his sparring partner – and my accuser is my sparring partner. He trains me in patience, civility and even temper.

A brief existence is common to all things, and yet you avoid and pursue all things as if they would be eternal.

A key point to bear in mind: The value of attentiveness varies in proportion to its object. You're better off not giving the small things more time than they deserve.

A man must learn a great deal to enable him to pass a correct judgment on another man's acts.

A man should be upright, not be kept upright.

A man when he has done a good act, does not call out for others to come and see, but he goes on to another act, as a vine goes on to produce again the grapes in season.

A man's worth is no greater than his ambitions.

A noble man compares and estimates himself by an idea which is higher than himself; and a mean man, by one lower than himself. The one produces aspiration; the other ambition, which is the way in which a vulgar man aspires.

A person's worth is measured by the worth of what he values.

A setback has often cleared the way for greater prosperity. Many things have fallen only to rise to more exalted heights.

A thing is neither better nor worse for having been praised.

A vine cannot behave olively, nor an olive tree vinely – it is impossible, inconceivable. No more can a human being wholly efface his native disposition.

Abstinence, not only from evil deeds, but even from evil thoughts; and further, simplicity in my way of living, far removed from the habits of the rich.

Accept the things to which fate binds you, and love the people with whom fate brings you together, but do so with all your heart.

Accept whatever comes to you woven in the pattern of your destiny, for what could more aptly fit your needs?

Accustom yourself to attend carefully to what is said by another, and as much as it is possible, try to inhabit the speaker's mind.

Acquire the contemplative way of seeing how all things change into one another, and constantly attend to it, and exercise yourself about this part of philosophy. For nothing is so much adapted to produce magnanimity.

Adapt yourself to the things among which your lot has been cast and love sincerely the fellow creatures with whom destiny has ordained that you shall live.

All disturbances arise solely from the opinions within us.

All our efforts must be directed towards an end, or we will act in vain. If it is not the right end, we will fail utterly.

All things are changing: and you yourself are in continuous mutation and in a manner in continuous destruction, and the whole universe, too.

All you need are these: certainty of judgment in the present moment; action for the common good in the present moment; and an attitude of gratitude in the present moment for anything that comes your way.

Almost nothing material is needed for a happy life, for he who has understood existence.

Altogether the interval is small between birth and death; and consider with how much trouble, and in company with what sort of people and in what a feeble body, this interval is laboriously passed.

Always observe how ephemeral and worthless human things are, and what was yesterday a speck of semen tomorrow will be a mummy or ashes.

Ambition means tying your well-being to what other people say or do. Self-indulgence means tying it to the things that happen to you. Sanity means tying it to your own actions.

An ignorant person is inclined to blame others for his own misfortune. To blame oneself is proof of progress. But the wise man never has to blame another or himself.

And thou wilt give thyself relief, if thou doest every act of thy life as if it were the last.

Anger cannot be dishonest.

Another person will not hurt you without your cooperation; you are hurt the moment you believe yourself to be.

Another thing which will help you is to turn your mind to other thoughts and that way get away from your suffering. Call to mind things which you have done that have been upright or courageous; run over in your mind the finest parts you have played.

Anything in any way beautiful derives its beauty from itself and asks nothing beyond itself. Praise is no part of it, for nothing is made worse or better by praise.

As an antidote to battle unkindness we were given kindness.

As if you had died and your life had extended only to this present moment, use the surplus that is left to you to live from this time onward according to nature.

As it is with a play, so it is with life – what matters is not how long the acting lasts, but how good it is. It is not important at what point you stop. Stop wherever you will – only make sure that you round it off with a good ending.

As the same fire assumes different shapes when it consumes objects differing in shape, so does the one self take the shape of every creature in whom he is present.

As you are careful when you walk not to step on a nail or turn your ankle, so you should take care not to do any injury to your character at the same time.

At dawn, when you have trouble getting out of bed, tell yourself: "I have to go to work — as a human being. What do I have to complain of, if I'm going to do what I was born for — the things I was brought into the world to do? Or is this what I was created for? To huddle under the blankets and stay warm?"

Be cheerful also, and do not seek external help or the tranquility that others give. A man then must stand erect, not be kept erect by others.

Be content with what you are, and wish not change; nor dread your last day, nor long for it.

Be like the promontory against which the waves continually break; but it stands firm and tames the fury of the water around it.

Bear in mind that everything that exists is already fraying at the edges, and in transition, subject to fragmentation and to rot. Or that everything was born to die.

Because a thing seems difficult for you, do not think it impossible for anyone to accomplish.

Because we're the only animals who not only die but are conscious of it even while it happens, we are beset by anxiety.

Because what is a human being? Part of a community – the community of gods and men, primarily, and secondarily that of the city we happen to inhabit, which is only a microcosm of the universe in toto.

Before long, nature, which controls it all, will alter everything you see and use it as material for something else – over and over again. So that the world is continually renewed.

Begin – to begin is half the work, let half still remain; again, begin this, and thou wilt have finished.

Being attached to many things, we are weighed down and dragged along with them.

Brief is man's life and small the nook of the earth where he lives; brief, too, is the longest posthumous fame, buoyed only by a succession of poor human beings who will very soon die and who know little of themselves, much less of someone who died long ago.

But if you accept the obstacle and work with what you're given, an alternative will present itself – another piece of what you're trying to assemble. Action by action.

Conceal a flaw, and the world will imagine the worst.

Confine yourself to the present.

Consider at what price you sell your integrity; but please, for God's sake, don't sell it cheap.

Consider how much more you often suffer from your anger and grief, than from those very things for which you are angry and grieved.

Consider if you have behaved to all in such a way that this way be said of you: Never has he wronged a man in deed or word.

Consider that as the heaps of sand piled on one another hide the former sands, so in life the events that go before are soon covered by those that come after.

Consider that before long you will be nobody and nowhere, nor will any of the things exist that you now see, nor any of those who are now living. For all things are formed by nature to change and be turned and to perish in order that other things in continuous succession may exist.

Consider that everything is opinion, and opinion is in your power. Take away then, when you choose, your opinion, and like a mariner who has rounded the headland, you will find calm, everything stable, and a waveless bay.

Consider that you also do many things wrong, and that you are a man like others; and even if you do abstain from certain faults, still you have the disposition to commit them, though either through cowardice, or concern about reputation, or some such mean motive, you abstain from such faults.

Consider what men are when they are eating, sleeping, coupling, evacuating, and so forth. Then what kind of men they are when they are imperious and arrogant, or angry and scolding from their elevated place.

Constantly and, if it be possible, on the occasion of every impression on the soul, apply to it the principles of physics, ethics, and logic.

Constantly recall those who have complained greatly about anything, those who have been most conspicuous by the greatest fame or misfortunes or enmities or fortunes of any kind: then think, where are they all now? Smoke and ash and a tale, or not even a tale.

Death and life, honor and dishonor, pain and pleasure — all these things equally happen to good men and bad, being things which make us neither better nor worse. Therefore, they are neither good nor evil.

Death and life, success and failure, pain and pleasure, wealth and poverty, all these happen to good and bad alike, and they are neither noble nor shameful – and hence neither good nor bad.

Death and pain are not frightening, it's the fear of pain and death we need to fear. Which is why we praise the poet who wrote, 'Death is not fearful, but dying like a coward is.'

Death is a release from the impressions of the senses, and from desires that make us their puppets, and from the vagaries of the mind, and from the hard service of the flesh.

Death is necessary and cannot be avoided. I mean, where am I going to go to get away from it?

Death is not an evil. What is it then? The one law mankind has that is free of all discrimination.

Death, like birth, is a secret of Nature.

Death. The end of sense-perception, of being controlled by our emotions, of mental activity, of enslavement to our bodies.

Despise not death, but welcome it, for nature wills it like all else.

Discard your misperceptions. Stop being jerked like a puppet. Limit yourself to the present.

Do as Socrates did, never replying to the question of where he was from with, 'I am Athenian,' or 'I am from Corinth,' but always, 'I am a citizen of the world.'

Do every act of your life as if it were your last.

Do little, if you want contentment of mind.

Do not act as if you were going to live ten thousand years. Death hangs over you. While you live, while it is in your power, be good.

Do not be perturbed, for all things are according to the nature of the universal; and in a little time, you will be nobody and nowhere.

Do not be whirled about, but in every movement have respect to justice, and on the occasion of every impression maintain the faculty of comprehension or understanding.

Do not indulge in dreams of having what you have not, but reckon up the chief of the blessings you do possess, and then thankfully remember how you would crave for them if they were not yours.

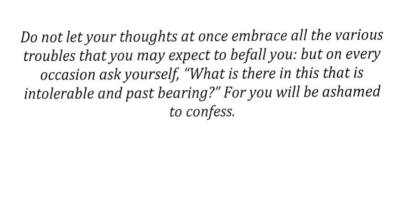

Do not let your thoughts at once embrace all the various troubles that you may expect to befall you: but on every occasion ask yourself, "What is there in this that is intolerable and past bearing?" For you will be ashamed to confess.

Do not waste what remains of your life in speculating about your neighbors, unless with a view to some mutual benefit. To wonder what so-and-so is doing and why, or what he is saying, or thinking, or scheming – in a word, anything that distracts you from fidelity to the ruler within you – means a loss of opportunity for some other task.

Do you have reason? I have. Why then do you not use it?

Do you want to know if you are educated? Show us your values, philosopher.

Does what's happened keep you from acting with justice, generosity, self-control, sanity, prudence, honesty, humility, straightforwardness, and all other qualities that allow a person's nature to fulfill itself? So remember this principle when something threatens to cause you pain: the thing itself was no misfortune at all; to endure it and prevail is great good fortune.

Don't be ashamed to need help. Like a soldier storming a wall, you have a mission to accomplish. And if you've been wounded and you need a comrade to pull you up? So what?

Don't be disappointed if you return home with the very same set of ideas you arrived with. Because you had no intention of changing, correcting or adopting others in their place.

Don't be overheard complaining... Not even to yourself.

Don't believe your situation is genuinely bad – no one can make you do that. Is there smoke in the house? If it's not suffocating, I will stay indoors; if it proves too much, I'll leave. Always remember – the door is open.

Don't hope that events will turn out the way you want, welcome events in whichever way they happen: this is the path to peace.

Don't let outward appearances mislead you into thinking that someone with more prestige, power or some other distinction must on that account be happy.

Don't waste the rest of your time here worrying about other people – unless it affects the common good. It will keep you from doing anything useful. You'll be too preoccupied with what so-and-so is doing, and why, and what they're saying, and what they're thinking, and what they're up to, and all the other things that throw you off and keep you from focusing on your own mind.

Drunkenness inflames and lays bare every vice, removing the reserve that acts as a chuck on impulses to wrong behaviour.

Dwell on the beauty of life. Watch the stars, and see yourself running with them.

Each day provides its own gifts.

Each thing is of like form from everlasting and comes around again in its cycle.

Either all things proceed from one intelligent source and come together as in one body, and the part ought not to find fault with what is done for the benefit of the whole; or there are only atoms, and nothing else than mixture and dispersion. Why, then, are you disturbed?

Either you're going to be depressed when your wish is not realized or foolishly pleased with yourself if it is, overjoyed for the wrong reasons.

Enough of this miserable, whining life. Stop monkeying around! Why are you troubled? What's new here? What's so confounding? The one responsible? Take a good look. Or just the matter itself? Then look at that. There's nothing else to look at. And as far as the gods go, by now you could try being more straightforward and kind. It's the same, whether you've examined these things for a hundred years, or only three.

Even the smallest thing should be done with reference to an end.

Every day as it comes should be welcomed and reduced forthwith into our own possession as if it were the finest day imaginable. What flies past has to be seized at.

Every part of me then will be reduced by change into some part of the universe, and that again will change into another part of the universe, and so on forever.

Everything that exists is in a manner the seed of that which will be.

Everything that happens happens as it should, and if you observe carefully, you will find this to be so.

Everything we hear is an opinion, not a fact. Everything we see is a perspective, not the truth.

Failure to observe what is in the mind of another has seldom made a man unhappy; but those who do not observe the movements of their own minds must of necessity be unhappy.

Finally, waiting for death with a cheerful mind, as being nothing else than a dissolution of the elements of which every living being is compounded. But if there is no harm to the elements themselves in each continually changing into another, why should a man have any apprehension about the change and dissolution of all the elements?

First, do nothing inconsiderately or without a purpose. Second, make your acts refer to nothing else but a social end.

For all their compliments do verses pay? They mayn't, yet these same poems make me gay.

For God's sake, stop honouring externals, quit turning yourself into the tool of mere matter, or of people who can supply you or deny you those material things.

For what does reason purport to do? "Establish what is true, eliminate what is false and suspend judgement in doubtful cases".

For where else is friendship found if not with fairness, reliability and respect for virtue only?

Forget everything else. Keep hold of this alone and remember it: Each of us lives only now, this brief instant. The rest has been lived already, or is impossible to see.

Forward, as occasion offers. Never look round to see whether any shall note it... Be satisfied with success in even the smallest matter, and think that even such a result is no trifle.

From Maximus I learned self-government, and not to be led aside by anything; and cheerfulness in all circumstances, as well as in illness.

From my brother Severus to love my kin, and to love truth, and to love justice.

Tolerate ignorant persons, and those who form opinions without consideration.

Give thyself time to learn something new and good, and cease to be whirled around.

Give yourself a gift: the present moment.

Glory paid to our ashes comes too late.

Glory's an empty, changeable thing, as fickle as the weather.

Have I been made for this, to lie under the blankets and keep myself warm?

Have I done something for the common good? Then I share in the benefits. To stay centered on that. Not to give up.

*He often acts unjustly who does not do a certain thing;
not only he who does a certain thing.*

*He who does wrong does wrong against himself. He who
acts unjustly acts unjustly to himself, because he makes
himself bad.*

*He who has a vehement desire for posthumous fame
does not consider that every one of those who remember
him will himself also die very soon.*

*He who is afraid of pain will sometimes also be afraid of
some of the things that will happen in the world, and
even this is impiety. And he who pursues pleasure will
not abstain from injustice, and this is plainly impiety.*

He who lives in harmony with himself lives in harmony with the universe.

Here is a rule to remember in future, when anything tempts you to feel bitter: not "This is misfortune," but "To bear this worthily is good fortune".

How easy it is to repel and to wipe away every impression which is troublesome or unsuitable, and immediately to be in all tranquility.

How long will you wait before you demand the best of yourself, and trust reason to determine what is best?

How much more grievous are the consequences of anger than the causes of it.

How much time he saves who does not look to see what his neighbor says or does or thinks.

How quickly things disappear: in the universe the bodies themselves, but in time the memory of them.

How ridiculous and how strange to be surprised at anything which happens in life.

How short is the time from birth to dissolution, and the illimitable time before birth as well as the equally boundless time after dissolution.

How small a part of the boundless and unfathomable time is assigned to every man! For it is very soon swallowed up in the eternal. And how small a part of the whole substance! And how small a part of the universal soul! And on what a small clod of the whole earth you creep!

How soon will time cover all things, and how many it has covered already.

How strangely men act. They will not praise those who are living at the same time and living with themselves; but to be themselves praised by posterity, by those whom they have never seen or ever will see, this they set much value on.

How trivial the things we want so passionately are.

I cannot escape death, but at least I can escape the fear of it.

I do what is mine to do; the rest doesn't disturb me. The rest is inanimate, or has no logos, or it wanders at random and has lost the road.

I have often wondered how it is that every man loves himself more than all the rest of men, but yet sets less value on his own opinions of himself than on the opinions of others.

I say that virtue is more valuable than wealth to the same degree that eyes are more valuable than fingernails.

I see no virtue that is opposed to justice; but I see a virtue that is opposed to love of pleasure, and that is temperance.

If a man is mistaken, instruct him kindly and show him his error. But if you are not able, blame yourself, or not even yourself.

If any man is able to convince me and show me that I do not think or act right, I will gladly change; for I seek the truth by which no man was ever injured. But he is injured who abides in his error and ignorance.

If it's not right, don't do it. If it's not true, don't say it.

If money is your only standard, then consider that, by your lights, someone who loses their nose does not suffer any harm.

If someone is able to show me that what I think or do is not right, I will happily change, for I seek the truth, by which no one was ever truly harmed. It is the person who continues in his self-deception and ignorance who is harmed.

If someone is incapable of distinguishing good things from bad and neutral things from either – well, how could such a person be capable of love? The power to love, then, belongs only to the wise man.

If something does not make a person worse in himself, neither does it make his life worse, nor does it harm him without or within.

If then there is an invincible necessity, why do you resist?

If they've injured you, then they're the ones who suffer for it. But have they?

If we try to adapt our mind to the regular sequence of changes and accept the inevitable with good grace, our life will proceed quite smoothly and harmoniously.

If you are distressed by anything external, the pain is not due to the thing itself, but to your estimate of it; and this you have the power to revoke at any moment.

If you are pained by any external thing, it is not this thing that disturbs you, but your own judgment about it. And it is in your power to wipe out this judgment now.

If you are pained by external things, it is not they that disturb you, but your own judgement of them. And it is in your power to wipe out that judgement now.

If you commit to philosophy, be prepared at once to be laughed at and made the butt of many snide remarks.

If you didn't learn these things in order to demonstrate them in practice, what did you learn them for?

If you don't want to be cantankerous, don't feed your temper, or multiply incidents of anger. Suppress the first impulse to be angry, then begin to count the days on which you don't get mad.

If you have been placed in a position above others, are you automatically going to behave like a despot? Remember who you are and whom you govern – that they are kinsmen, brothers by nature, fellow descendants of Zeus.

If you learn that someone is speaking ill of you, don't try to defend yourself against the rumours; respond instead with, 'Yes, and he doesn't know the half of it, because he could have said more'.

If you like doing something, do it regularly; if you don't like doing something, make a habit of doing something different. The same goes for moral inclinations. When you get angry, you should know that you aren't guilty of an isolated lapse, you've encouraged a trend and thrown fuel on the fire.

If you lost the capacity to read, or play music, you would think it was a disaster, but you think nothing of losing the capacity to be honest, decent and civilized.

If you seek tranquility, do less. Or do what's essential – what the logos of a social being requires, and in the requisite way. Which brings a double satisfaction: to do less, better. Because most of what we say and do is not essential. If you can eliminate it, you'll have more time, and more tranquility. Ask yourself at every moment, 'Is this necessary?'

If you shall be afraid not because you must some time cease to live, but if you shall fear never to have begun to live according to nature – then you will be a man worthy of the universe that has produced you, and you will cease to be a stranger in your native land.

If you want to be a man of honour and a man of your word, who is going to stop you? You say you don't want to be obstructed or forced to do something against your will – well, who is going to force you to desire things that you don't approve, or dislike something against your better judgement?

If, at some point in your life, you should come across anything better than justice, honesty, self-control, courage – than a mind satisfied that is has succeeded in enabling you to act rationally, and satisfied to accept what's beyond its control – if you find anything better than that, embrace it without reservations – it must be an extraordinary thing indeed – and enjoy it to the full.

In a little while you will have forgotten everything; in a little while everything will have forgotten you.

In a word, if there is a god, all is well; and if chance rules, do not also be governed by it.

In like manner view also the other epochs of time and of whole nations, and see how many after great efforts soon fell and were resolved into the elements.

In the morning, when you rise unwillingly, let this thought be present: I am rising to the work of a human being.

In whatever I do, either by myself or with another, I must direct my energies to this alone, that it shall conduce to the common interest and be in harmony with it.

In your conversation, don't dwell at excessive length on your own deeds or adventures. Just because you enjoy recounting your exploits doesn't mean that others derive the same pleasure from hearing about them.

Injustice is impiety. For since the universal nature has made rational animals for the sake of one another to help one another according to their deserts, but in no way to injure one another, he who transgresses her will is clearly guilty of impiety toward the highest divinity.

Is a world without shameless people possible? No. So this person you've just met is one of them. Get over it.

Is any man afraid of change? What can take place without change? What then is more pleasing or more suitable to the universal nature? And can you take a hot bath unless the wood for the fire undergoes a change? And can you be nourished unless the food undergoes a change? And can anything else that is useful be accomplished without change? Do you not see then that for yourself also to change is just the same, and equally necessary for the universal nature?

Is helping others less valuable to you? Not worth your effort?

It is a proper work of a man to be benevolent to his own kind, to despise the movements of the senses, to form a just judgment of plausible appearances, and to take a survey of the nature of the universe and of the things that happen in it.

It is in no man's power to have whatever he wants; but he has it in his power not to wish for what he hasn't got, and cheerfully make the most of the things that do come his way.

It is in our power to have no opinion about a thing and not to be disturbed in our soul; for things themselves have no natural power to form our judgments.

It is in your power to live here. But if men do not permit you, then get away out of life, as if you were suffering no harm. The house is smoky, and I quit it. Why do you think that this is any trouble? But so long as nothing of the kind drives me out, I remain, am free, and no man shall hinder me from doing what I choose; and I choose to do what is according to the nature of the rational and social animal.

It is in your power whenever you choose to retire into yourself. For there is no retreat that is quieter or freer from trouble than a man's own soul.

It is just charming how people boast about qualities beyond their control. For instance, 'I am better than you because I have many estates, while you are practically starving'; or, 'I'm a consul,' 'I'm a governor,' or 'I have fine curly hair.'

It is not death that a man should fear, but he should fear never beginning to live.

It is not right that anything of any other kind, such as praise from the many, or power, or enjoyment of pleasure, should come into competition with that which is rationally and politically and practically good.

It is our own opinions that disturb us. Take away these opinions then, and resolve to dismiss your judgment about an act as if it were something grievous, and your anger is gone.

It stares you in the face. No role is so well suited to philosophy as the one you happen to be in right now.

It will even do to socialize with men of good character, in order to model your life on theirs, whether you choose someone living or someone from the past.

It's silly to try to escape other people's faults. They are inescapable. Just try to escape your own.

It's time you realized that you have something in you more powerful and miraculous than the things that affect you and make you dance like a puppet.

Just ask whether they put their self-interest in externals or in moral choice. If it's in externals, you cannot call them friends, any more than you can call them trustworthy, consistent, courageous or free.

Just prove to me that you are trustworthy, high-minded and reliable, and that your intentions are benign – prove to me that your jar doesn't have a hole in it – and you'll find that I won't even wait for you to open your heart to me, I'll be the first to implore you to lend an ear to my own affairs.

Just that you do the right thing. The rest doesn't matter.

Justice will not be observed, if we either care for indifferent things or are easily deceived and careless and changeable.

Keep at it... As a blazing fire takes whatever you throw on it, and makes it light and flame.

Keep in mind how fast things pass by and are gone – those that are now and those to come. Existence flows past us like a river: the 'what' is in constant flux, the 'why' has a thousand variations. Nothing is stable, not even what's right here. The infinity of past and future gapes before us – a chasm whose depths we cannot see.

Keep reminding yourself of the way things are connected, of their relatedness. All things are implicated in one another and in sympathy with each other. This event is the consequence of some other one. Things push and pull on each other, and breathe together, and are one.

Labor willingly and diligently, undistracted and aware of the common interest.

Let it happen, if it wants, to whatever it can happen to. And what's affected can complain about it if it wants. It doesn't hurt me unless I interpret its happening as harmful to me. I can choose not to.

Let it make no difference to you whether you are cold or warm, if you are doing your duty; and whether you are drowsy or satisfied with sleep; and whether ill-spoken of or praised; and whether dying or doing something else.

Let men see, let them know, a real man, who lives as he was meant to live.

Let not your mind run on what you lack as much as on what you have already.

Let us overlook many things in those who are like antagonists in the gymnasium. For it is in our power, as I said, to get out of the way and to have no suspicion or hatred.

Life is neither good or evil, but only a place for good and evil.

Life is short. That's all there is to say. Get what you can from the present – thoughtfully, justly.

Life is warfare... Then what can guide us? Only philosophy.

Live a good life. If there are gods and they are just, then they will not care how devout you have been, but will welcome you based on the virtues you have lived by. If there are gods, but unjust, then you should not want to worship them. If there are no gods, then you will be gone, but will have lived a noble life that will live on in the memories of your loved ones.

Live out your life in truth and justice, tolerant of those who are neither true nor just.

*Look back over the past, with its changing empires that
rose and fell, and you can foresee the future, too.*

*Look not round at the depraved morals of others, but
run straight along the line without deviating from it.*

*Look well into thyself; there is a source of strength
which will always spring up if thou wilt always look.*

*Look within. Within is the foundation of good, and it will
ever bubble up, if you will ever dig.*

Loss is nothing else but change, and change is Nature's delight.

Mastery of reading and writing requires a master. Still, more so life.

Misfortune nobly born is good fortune.

Most of us dread the deadening of the body and will do anything to avoid it. About the deadening of the soul, however, we don't care one iota.

My advice is really this: what we hear the philosophers saying and what we find in their writings should be applied in our pursuit of the happy life. We should hunt out the helpful pieces of teaching, and the spirited and noble-minded sayings which are capable of immediate practical application – not far-fetched or archaic expressions or extravagant metaphors and figures of speech – and learn them so well that words become works.

My city and country, so far as I am Antoninus, is Rome; but so far as I am a man, it is the world.

Never get into family fights over material things; give them up willingly, and your moral standing will increase in proportion.

Never let the future disturb you. You will meet it, if you have to, with the same weapons of reason which today arm you against the present.

Never value anything as profitable that compels you to break your promise, to lose your self-respect, to hate any man, to suspect, to curse, to act the hypocrite, to desire anything that needs walls and curtains.

No man can escape his destiny, the next inquiry being how he may best live the time that he has to live.

No matter what anyone says or does, my task is to be good.

No one objects to what is useful to him. To be of use to others is natural. Then don't object to what is useful to you – being of use.

No role is so well suited to philosophy as the one you happen to be in right now.

No time for reading. For controlling your arrogance, yes. For overcoming pain and pleasure, yes. For outgrowing ambition, yes. For not feeling anger at stupid and unpleasant people – even for caring about them – for that, yes.

Not to live as if you had endless years ahead of you. Death overshadows you. While you're alive and able – be good.

Nothing happens to anyone that he can't endure.

Nothing has such power to broaden the mind as the ability to investigate systematically and truly all that comes under thy observation in life.

Nothing important comes into being overnight; even grapes or figs need time to ripen. If you say that you want a fig now, I will tell you to be patient. First, you must allow the tree to flower, then put forth fruit; then you have to wait until the fruit is ripe. So if the fruit of a fig tree is not brought to maturity instantly or in an hour, how do you expect the human mind to come to fruition, so quickly and easily?

Nothing is as encouraging as when virtues are visibly embodied in the people around us, when we're practically showered with them.

Nothing is burdensome if taken lightly, and how nothing need arouse one's irritation so long as one doesn't make it bigger than it is by getting irritated.

Nothing should be done without a purpose.

Now it is in my power to let no badness be in this soul, nor desire nor any perturbation at all; but looking at all things, I see their true nature, and I use each according to its value.

Now think of the things which goad man into destroying man: they are hope, envy, hatred, fear and contempt.

Nowhere can man find a quieter or more untroubled retreat than in his own soul.

Objective judgement, now, at this very moment. Unselfish action, now, at this very moment. Willing acceptance, now, at this very moment – of all external events. That's all you need.

Observe always that everything is the result of change, and get used to thinking that there is nothing nature loves so well as to change existing forms and make new ones like them.

Observe constantly that all things take place by change, and accustom thyself to consider that the nature of the Universe loves nothing so much as to change the things which are, and to make new things like them.

Often injustice lies in what you aren't doing, not only in what you are doing.

On the occasion of every act ask yourself, "How is this with respect to me? Will I regret it? A little time and I am dead, and all is gone".

One thing here is worth a great deal: to pass your life in truth and justice, with a benevolent disposition even to liars and unjust men.

One thing I know: all the works of mortal man lie under sentence of mortality; we live among things that are destined to perish.

Only attend to yourself, and resolve to be a good man in every act that you do.

Or is it your reputation that's bothering you? But look at how soon we're all forgotten. The abyss of endless time that swallows it all. The emptiness of those applauding hands. The people who praise us; how capricious they are, how arbitrary. And the tiny region it takes place. The whole earth a point in space – and most of it uninhabited.

Others have been plundered, indiscriminately, set upon, betrayed, beaten up, attacked with poison or with calumny – mention anything you like, it has happened to plenty of people.

Our anger and annoyance are more detrimental to us than the things themselves which anger or annoy us.

Our life is what our thoughts make it.

Pain is neither intolerable nor everlasting if you bear in mind that it has its limits, and if you add nothing to it in imagination.

Pain too is just a scary mask: look under it and you will see. The body sometimes suffers, but relief is never far behind. And if that isn't good enough for you, the door stands open; otherwise put up with it. The door needs to stay open whatever the circumstances, with the result that our problems disappear.

Passions stem from frustrated desire.

People exist for one another. You can instruct or endure them.

People look for retreats for themselves, in the country, by the coast, or in the hills... There is nowhere that a person can find a more peaceful and trouble-free retreat than in his own mind... So constantly give yourself this retreat, and renew yourself.

People who are physically ill are unhappy with a doctor who doesn't give them advice, because they think he has given up on them. Shouldn't we feel the same towards a philosopher – and assume that he has given up hope of our ever becoming rational – if he will no longer tell us what we need (but may not like) to hear?

People who love what they do wear themselves down doing it, they even forget to wash or eat.

People with a strong physical constitution can tolerate extremes of hot and cold; people of strong mental health can handle anger, grief, joy and the other emotions.

Perfect tranquility within consists in the good ordering of the mind, the realm of your own.

Perfection of character is this: to live each day as if it were your last, without frenzy, without apathy, without pretence.

Perhaps the desire of the thing called fame torments you. See how soon everything is forgotten, and look at the chaos of infinite time on each side of the present, and the emptiness of applause, and the fickleness and lack of judgment in those who pretend to give praise, and the narrowness of its domain, and be quiet at last.

Perhaps there are none more lazy, or more truly ignorant, than your everlasting readers.

Pleasures, when they go beyond a certain limit, are but punishments.

Poverty is the mother of crime.

Poverty's no evil to anyone unless he kicks against it.

Practice really hearing what people say. Do your best to get inside their minds.

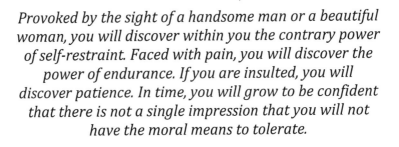

Provoked by the sight of a handsome man or a beautiful woman, you will discover within you the contrary power of self-restraint. Faced with pain, you will discover the power of endurance. If you are insulted, you will discover patience. In time, you will grow to be confident that there is not a single impression that you will not have the moral means to tolerate.

Receive wealth or prosperity without arrogance; and be ready to let it go.

Receive without pride, let go without attachment.

Refer your action to no other end than the common good.

Reflect on the other social roles you play. If you are a council member, consider what a council member should do. If you are young, what does being young mean, if you are old, what does age imply, if you are a father, what does fatherhood entail? Each of our titles, when reflected upon, suggests the acts appropriate to it.

Remember this, that there is a proper dignity and proportion to be observed in the performance of every act of life.

Remember to act always as if you were at a symposium. When the food or drink comes around, reach out and take some politely; if it passes you by don't try pulling it back. And if it has not reached you yet, don't let your desire run ahead of you, be patient until your turn comes.

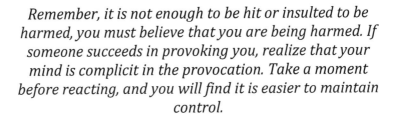

Remember, it is not enough to be hit or insulted to be harmed, you must believe that you are being harmed. If someone succeeds in provoking you, realize that your mind is complicit in the provocation. Take a moment before reacting, and you will find it is easier to maintain control.

Remember, too, on every occasion that leads you to vexation to apply this principle: not that this is a misfortune, but that to bear it nobly is good fortune.

Remind yourself that it is not the future or what has passed that afflicts you, but always the present.

Resolve to accept whatever happens as necessary and familiar, flowing like water from that same source and spring.

Say to yourself each time, 'He did what he believed was right.' (When someone does something you don't like)

Set yourself in motion, if it is in your power, and do not look about you to see if anyone will observe it; nor yet expect Plato's Republic: but be content if the smallest thing goes on well, and consider such an event to be no small matter.

Settle on the type of person you want to be and stick to it, whether alone or in company.

Shall any man hate me? That will be his affair. But I will be mild and benevolent toward every man, and ready to show even him his mistake, not reproachfully, nor yet as making a display of my endurance, but nobly and honestly.

Show me one person who cares how they act, someone for whom success is less important than the manner in which it is achieved. While out walking, who gives any thought to the act of walking itself? Who pays attention to the process of planning, not just the outcome?

Show me someone untroubled with disturbing thoughts about illness, danger, death, exile or loss of reputation. By all the gods, I want to see a Stoic!

Since it is possible that you might depart from life this very moment, regulate every act and thought accordingly.

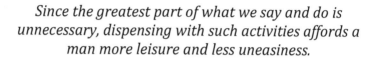

Since the greatest part of what we say and do is unnecessary, dispensing with such activities affords a man more leisure and less uneasiness.

So does this misfortune prevent you in any way from being just, generous, sober, reasonable, careful, free from error, courteous, free, etc. – all of which together make human nature complete?

So I look for the best and am prepared for the opposite.

So there is the comforting thing about extremities of pain: if you feel it too much you are bound to stop feeling it.

So when you hear that even life and the like are indifferent, don't become apathetic; and by the same token, when you're advised to care about them, don't become superficial and conceive a passion for externals.

So you were born to feel "nice"? Instead of doing things and experiencing them? Don't you see the plants, the birds, the ants and spiders and bees going about their individual tasks, putting the world in order, as best they can? And you're not willing to do your job as a human being? Why aren't you running to do what your nature demands?

Someone bathes in haste; don't say he bathes badly, but in haste. Someone drinks a lot of wine; don't say he drinks badly, but a lot. Until you know their reasons, how do you know that their actions are vicious?

Something good should be a source of pride, correct? 'Yes.' And can one really take pride in a momentary pleasure? Please don't say yes.

Speaking for myself, I hope death overtakes me when I'm occupied solely with the care of my character, in an effort to make it passionless, free, unrestricted and unrestrained.

Stick to what's in front of you – idea, action, utterance.

Stick with the situation at hand, and ask, "Why is this so unbearable? Why can't I endure it?" You'll be embarrassed to answer.

Stop allowing yourself your mind to be a slave, to be jerked about by selfish impulses, to kick against fate and the present, and to mistrust the future.

Stop wishing for something else to happen, for a different fate. That is to live a false life.

Straight, not straightened.

Such as are your habitual thoughts, such also will be the character of your mind.

*Take a good hard look at people's ruling principle,
especially of the wise, what they run away from and
what they seek out.*

*Take care that you don't treat inhumanity as it treats
human beings.*

*Take me and cast me where you will; for there I shall
keep my divine part tranquil, that is, content, if it can
feel and act conformably to its proper constitution.*

*Take the shortest route, the one that nature planned –
to speak and act in the healthiest way. Do that, and be
free of pain and stress, free of all calculation and
pretention.*

That which is not good for the bee-hive cannot be good for the bees.

The act of dying is one of the acts of life.

The art of life is more like the wrestler's art than the dancer's, in respect of this, that it should stand ready and firm to meet onsets that are sudden and unexpected.

The art of living is more like wrestling than dancing.

The best revenge is not to be like your enemy.

The best way to avenge yourself is to not be like that.

The first rule is to keep an untroubled spirit. The second is to look things in the face and know them for what they are.

The first step: Don't be anxious. Nature controls it all.

The first thing a pretender to philosophy must do is get rid of their presuppositions; a person is not going to undertake to learn anything that they think they already know.

The flaw which is hidden is deemed greater than it is.

The following are non-sequiturs: 'I am richer, therefore superior to you'; or 'I am a better speaker, therefore a better person, than you'.

The gods are not to blame. They do nothing wrong, on purpose or by accident. Nor men either; they don't do it on purpose. No one is to blame.

The happiness of your life depends upon the quality of your thoughts: therefore, guard accordingly, and take care that you entertain no notions unsuitable to virtue and reasonable nature.

The history of your life is now complete and your service is ended: and how many beautiful things you have seen; and how many pleasures and pains you have despised; and how many things called honorable you have spurned; and to how many ill-minded folks you have shown a kind disposition.

The impediment to action advances action. What stands in the way becomes the way.

The love of power or money or luxurious living are not the only things which are guided by popular thinking. We take our cue from people's thinking even in the way we feel pain.

The man who spends his time choosing one resort after another in a hunt for peace and quiet, will in every place he visits find something to prevent him from relaxing.

The mind in itself has no needs, except for those it creates itself. Is undisturbed, except for its own disturbances. Knows no obstructions, except those from within.

The mind maintains its own tranquility by retiring into itself, and the ruling faculty is not made worse. But the parts that are harmed by pain, let them, if they can, give their opinion about it.

The mind that is free from passions is a citadel, for man has nothing more secure to which he can fly for refuge and repel every attack.

The object in life is not to be on the side of the majority, but to escape finding oneself in the ranks of the insane.

The only wealth which you will keep forever is the wealth you have given away.

The operations of the will are in our power; not in our power are the body, the body's parts, property, parents, siblings, children, country or friends.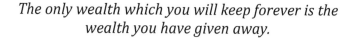

The perfection of moral character consists in this, in passing every day as if it were the last, and in being neither violently excited nor torpid nor playing the hypocrite.

The present is the only thing of which a man can be deprived, if it is true that this is the only thing which he has, and that a man cannot lose something he does not already possess.

The rational animal is consequently also a social animal.

The second step: Concentrate on what you have to do. Fix your eyes on it. Remind yourself that your task is to be a good human being; remind yourself what nature demands of people. Then do it, without hesitation, and speak the truth as you see it. But with kindness. With humility. Without hypocrisy.

The secret of all victory lies in the organization of the non-obvious.

The sexual embrace can only be compared with music and with prayer.

The spiritual meaning of love is measured by what it can do. Love is meant to heal. Love is meant to renew. Love is meant to bring us closer to God.

The things that are essential are acquired with little bother; it is the luxuries that call for toil and effort.

The tranquility that comes when you stop caring what they say. Or think, or do. Only what you do.

The true man is revealed in difficult times. So when trouble comes, think of yourself as a wrestler whom God, like a trainer, has paired with a tough young buck. For what purpose? To turn you into Olympic-class material. But this is going to take some sweat to accomplish.

The universal order and the personal order are nothing but different expressions and manifestations of a common underlying principle.

The universe is transformation: life is opinion.

The work of philosophy is simple and modest. Do not draw me aside into pomposity.

The world is maintained by change – in the elements and in the things they compose. That should be enough for you; treat it as an axiom.

There are times when even to live is an act of bravery.

There were two vices much blacker and more serious than the rest: lack of persistence and lack of self-control... persist and resist.

Things do not touch the soul, for they are external and remain immovable; so our perturbations come only from our inner opinions.

Think continually that all kinds of men, pursuits, and nations are dead.

Think not disdainfully of death, but look on it with favor; for even death is one of the things that Nature wills.

Think not so much of what you lack as of what you have: but of the things that you have, select the best, and then reflect how eagerly you would have sought them if you did not have them.

Think of all the years passed by in which you said to yourself "I'll do it tomorrow," and how the gods have again and again granted you periods of grace of which you have not availed yourself. It is time to realize that you are a member of the Universe, that you are born of Nature itself, and to know that a limit has been set to your time. Use every moment wisely, to perceive your inner refulgence, or 'twill be gone and nevermore within your reach.

Think of yourself as dead. You have lived your life.
Now take what's left and live it properly.

This presumption that you possess knowledge of any use
has to be dropped before you approach philosophy –
just as if we were enrolling in a school of music or
mathematics.

This, then, is consistent with the character of a
reflecting man, to be neither careless nor impatient nor
contemptuous with respect to death, but to wait for it as
one of the operations of nature.

This, then, is the beginning of philosophy – an
awareness of one's own mental fitness.

Throw away your books; stop letting yourself be distracted.

To accept without arrogance, to let it go with indifference.

To be angry at something means you've forgotten: That everything that happens is natural. That the responsibility is theirs, not yours.

To be feared is to fear: no one has been able to strike terror into others and at the same time enjoy peace of mind himself.

To be sure, external things of whatever kind require skill in their use, but we must not grow attached to them; whatever they are, they should only serve for us to show how skilled we are in our handling of them.

To do harm is to do yourself harm. To do an injustice is to do yourself an injustice.

To expect punishment is to suffer it; and to earn it is to expect it.

To have contemplated human life for forty years is the same as to have contemplated it for ten thousand years. For what more will you see?

To live happily is an inward power of the soul.

To live in peace, immune to all compulsion. Let them scream whatever they want.

To live the good life: We have the potential for it. If we can learn to be indifferent to what makes no difference.

To move from one unselfish action to another with God in mind. Only there, delight and stillness.

To rest in these principles only: the one, that nothing will happen to me which is not conformable to the nature of the universe; and the other, that it is in my power never to act contrary to my god and daimon: for there is no man who will compel me to this.

To the gods I am indebted for having good grandfathers, good parents, a good sister, good teachers, good associates, good kinsmen and friends, nearly everything good. For all these [blessings in my life] require the help of the gods and fortune.

To the rational animal the same act is at once according to nature and according to reason.

To the wise, life is a problem; to the fool, a solution.

To understand the true quality of people, you must look into their minds, and examine their pursuits and aversions.

Today I escaped anxiety. Or no, I discarded it, because it was within me, in my own perceptions – not outside.

Today I have got out of all trouble, or rather I have cast out all trouble, for it was not outside, but within and in my opinions.

Tomorrow is nothing, today is too late; the good lived yesterday.

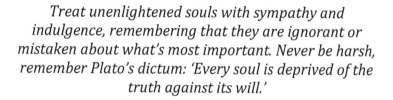

Treat unenlightened souls with sympathy and indulgence, remembering that they are ignorant or mistaken about what's most important. Never be harsh, remember Plato's dictum: 'Every soul is deprived of the truth against its will.'

Treat what you don't have as nonexistent. Look at what you have, the things you value most, and think of how much you'd crave them if you didn't have them. But be careful. Don't feel such satisfaction that you start to overvalue them – that it would upset you to lose them.

Treat whatever happens as wholly natural; not novel or hard to deal with; but familiar and easily handled.

True good fortune is what you make for yourself. Good fortune: good character, good intentions, good actions.

Turn your desire to stone. Quench your appetites. Keep your mind centered on itself.

Under no circumstances ever say 'I have lost something,' only 'I returned it.'

Very little is needed for everything to be upset and ruined, only a slight lapse in reason.

Very little is needed to make a happy life; it is all within yourself, in your way of thinking.

Waste no more time arguing about what a good man should be. Be one.

We are too much accustomed to attribute to a single cause that which is the product of several, and the majority of our controversies come from that.

We ought to do good to others as simply as a horse runs, or a bee makes honey, or a vine bears grapes season after season without thinking of the grapes it has borne.

We should discipline ourselves in small things, and from there progress to things of greater value. If you have a headache, practise not cursing. Don't curse every time you have an earache. And I'm not saying that you can't complain, only don't complain with your whole being.

What illusion about myself do I entertain?

*What is divine deserves our affection because it is good;
what is human deserves our affection because it is like
us.*

*What is the goal of virtue, after all, except a life that
flows smoothly?*

What is your art? To be good.

*What is your art? To be good. And how is this
accomplished well except by general principles, some*

about the nature of the universe, and others about the proper constitution of man?

What is your vocation? To be a good person.

What springs from earth dissolves to earth again, and heaven-born things fly to their native seat.

What then can guide a man? One thing and only one, philosophy. But this consists in keeping the daimon within a man free from violence and unharmed, superior to pains and pleasures, doing nothing without a purpose, nor yet falsely and with hypocrisy.

Whatever any one does or says, I must be good, just as if the emerald (or the gold or the purple) were always saying "Whatever any one does or says, I must be emerald and keep my color."

Whatever anyone does or says, I must be good, just as if the gold, or the emerald, or the purple were always saying this, whatever anyone does or says, I must be emerald and keep my color.

Whatever happens to you has been waiting to happen since the beginning of time.

Whatever man you meet with, immediately say to yourself: "What opinions has this man about good and bad?"

Whatever the nature of the whole does, and whatever serves to maintain it, is good for every part of nature.

Whatever the universal nature assigns to any man at any time is for the good of that man at that time.

When a guide meets up with someone who is lost, ordinarily his reaction is to direct him on the right path, not mock or malign him, then turn on his heel and walk away. As for you, lead someone to the truth and you will find that he can follow. But as long as you don't point it out to him, don't make fun of him; be aware of what you need to work on instead.

When another blames you or hates you, or people voice similar criticisms, go to their souls, penetrate inside and see what sort of people they are. You will realize that there is no need to be racked with anxiety that they should hold any particular opinion about you.

When another blames you or hates you, or when men say anything injurious about you, approach their poor souls, penetrate within, and see what kind of men they are. You will discover that there is no reason to be concerned that these men have this or that opinion about you.

When faced with anything painful or pleasurable, anything bringing glory or disrepute, realize that the crisis is now, that the Olympics have started, and waiting is no longer an option; that the chance for progress, to keep or lose, turns on the events of a single day.

When I see that one thing [virtue] is supreme and most important, I cannot say that something else is, just to make you happy.

When it comes to all we're required to go through, we're equals. No one is more vulnerable than the next man, and no one can be more sure of his surviving to the morrow.

When jarred, unavoidably, by circumstance, revert at once to yourself and don't lose the rhythm more than you can help. You'll have a better grasp of harmony if you keep going back to it.

When somebody's wife or child dies, to a man we all routinely say, 'Well, that's part of life.' But if one of our own family is involved, then right away it's 'Poor, poor me!' We would do better to remember how we react when a similar loss afflicts others.

When someone is properly grounded in life, they shouldn't have to look outside themselves for approval.

When they're really possessed by what they do, they'd rather stop eating and sleeping than give up practicing their arts.

When thou art above measure angry, bethink thee how momentary is man's life.

When you are offended at any man's fault, immediately turn to yourself and reflect in what manner you yourself have erred: for example, in thinking that money is a good thing or pleasure, or a bit of reputation, and the like.

When you arise in the morning, think of what a precious privilege it is to be alive – to breathe, to think, to enjoy, to love.

When you have assumed these names – good, modest, truthful, rational, a man of equanimity, and magnanimous – take care that you do not change these names; and if you should lose them, quickly return to them.

When you have been compelled by circumstances to be disturbed in a manner, quickly return to yourself and do not continue out of tune longer than the compulsion lasts.

When you have done a good act and another has received it, why do you look for a third thing besides these, as fools do, either to have the reputation of having done a good act or to obtain a return?

When you have trouble getting out of bed in the morning, remember that your defining characteristic – what defines a human being — is to work with others.

Even animals know how to sleep. And it's the characteristic activity that's the more natural one – more innate and more satisfying.

When you wake up in the morning, tell yourself: The people I deal with today will be meddling, ungrateful, arrogant, dishonest, jealous and surely... None of them can hurt me. Don't waste the rest of your time here worrying about other people... It will keep you from doing anything useful. Why do you not rather act than complain?

When you wish to delight yourself, think of the virtues of those who live with you; for instance, the activity of one, the modesty of another, the liberality of a third, and some other good quality of a fourth.

When you're called upon to speak, then speak, but never about banalities like gladiators, horses, sports, food and drink – common-place stuff. Above all don't gossip about people, praising, blaming or comparing them.

When you've done well and another has benefited by it, why like a fool do you look for a third thing on top— credit for the good deed or a favor in return?

Whenever anyone criticizes or wrongs you, remember that they are only doing or saying what they think is right. They cannot be guided by your views, only their own; so if their views are wrong, they are the ones who suffer insofar as they are misguided.

Whenever externals are more important to you than your own integrity, then be prepared to serve them the remainder of your life.

Whenever you are about to find fault with someone, ask yourself the following question: What fault of mine most nearly resembles the one I am about to criticize?

Where a man can live, he can also live well.

Whether it is a dispersion, or a resolution into atoms, or annihilation, it is either extinction or change.

Whether the universe is a concourse of atoms, or nature is a system, let this first be established: that I am a part of the whole that is governed by nature; next, that I stand in some intimate connection with other kindred parts.

While you live, while it is in your power, be good.

Who exactly are these people that you want to be admired by? Aren't they the same people you are in the habit of calling crazy? And is this your life ambition, then – to win the approval of lunatics?

Who wants to live with delusion and prejudice, being unjust, undisciplined, mean and ungrateful? 'No one.' No bad person, then, lives the way he wants, and no bad man is free.

Why are we still lazy, indifferent and dull? Why do we look for excuses to avoid training and exercising our powers of reason?

Why should we feel anger at the world? As if the world would notice?

WISE QUOTES: SOCRATES

With respect to what may happen to you from without, consider that it happens either by chance or according to Providence, and you must neither blame chance nor accuse Providence.

With what are you discontented? With the badness of men? Recall to your mind this conclusion, that rational animals exist for one another, and that to endure is a part of justice, and that men do wrong involuntarily.

Yes, you can – if you do everything as if it were the last thing you were doing in life, and stop being aimless, stop letting your emotions override what your mind tells you, stop being hypocritical, self-centered, irritable.

You always own the option of having no opinion. There is never any need to get worked up or to trouble your soul about things you can't control. These things are not asking to be judged by you. Leave them alone.

You are composed of three things: body, breath (life), intelligence. Of these the first two are yours insofar as it is your duty to take care of them; but the third alone is truly yours.

You can commit injustice by doing nothing.

*You can discard most of the junk that clutters your mind
– things that exist only there – and clear out space for
yourself: by comprehending the scale of the world, by
contemplating infinite time, by thinking of the speed
with which things change – each part of every thing; the
narrow space between our birth and death; the infinite
time before; the equality unbounded time that follows.*

*You can pass your life in an equable flow of happiness if
you can follow the right way and think and act in the
right way.*

*You could leave life right now. Let that determine what
you do and say and think.*

*You don't have to turn this into something. It doesn't
have to upset you. Things can't shape our decisions by
themselves.*

You don't love yourself enough. Or you'd love ~~y~~
nature too, and what it demands of you.

You have power over your mind – not outside events.
Realize this, and you will find strength.

You might as well get on your knees and pray that your
nose won't run. A better idea would be to wipe your
nose and forgo the prayer. The point is, isn't there
anything God gave you for your present problem?

You must become an old man in good time if you wish to
be an old man long.

realize, you take up very little space in the
.s a whole – your body, that is; in reason,
er, you yield to no one, not even to the gods,
reason is not measured in size but sense. So why
are for that side of you, where you and the gods are
equals?

You see how few things you have to do to live a
satisfying and reverent life? If you can manage this,
that's all even the gods can ask of you.

You will give yourself relief, if you do every act of your
life as if it were the last.

You're subject to sorrow, fear, jealousy, anger and
inconsistency. That's the real reason you should admit
that you are not wise.

Your life is short. You must turn to profit the pre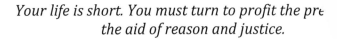
the aid of reason and justice.

Your mind will take the shape of what you frequently hold in thought, for the human spirit is colored by such impressions.

Your three components: body, breath, mind. Two are yours in trust; to the third alone you have clear title.

sent by

Printed in Great Britain
by Amazon